Endorsements

"Carlton's book *Reconsider: Could A Change in Your Perspective Change Your Life?* is his personal journey on how taking responsibility and altering your mindset can transform your life. This is a must read for all of us that have had challenges in our lives!" - Scott Sellers, Business Executive

"Looking at Mr. Perkins' perspective has always been a unique experience, but here we see that his thought process and conclusions cause one to pause and simply think. I love how he could take a simple concept and make it complex and vice versa. Two thumbs up!" - Laurence Gray, Chaplain and Pastor

"As I read this book about perspective, instead of a read, for me it was like Carlton carrying on a conversation with me. It's an easy read, informative and filled with many pearls of wisdom. It caused me to stop and reconsider my own perspective on some things. The chapter 'Exploring Relationships' where he explains some of the common reasons that people enter a relationship is spot on. He made it very straightforward to understand.

I love the point he makes in this chapter on Companionship being a common reason that people enter a relationship. "No matter how you define love, everyone longs for it. The caveat is that your perception of love affects your expectation, especially on the one whom you are relying on to give to you." This point is very true. Working with individuals in relationship coaching, through self-discovery one of the things that they learned about their relationship is that each had a different perspective of love of what their expectations were from each other. I thoroughly enjoyed each chapter and how he connected the natural with the spiritual.

If you want to change your life by reassessing your perspective, I recommend that you get yourself a copy of this book. It's food for thought. Great job Carlton! I am extremely proud of you, I love you." - Renee Morris, Life Coach — DARGANMORRIS Life Coaching, LLC

"Paradigm shift is what happened to me after reading this book. There was an understanding that overtook me, that challenged me to have a perspective of situations and life that would change lives and generations. This is the reason that I will absolutely recommend this read to anyone. Literally, it is more than self help, it is a legacy changer." - Crysta Marshall, Founder of Defined With Purpose

RECONSIDER

Could a Change in Perspective Change Your Life?

CARLTON PERKINS

LUCIDBOOKS

Table of Contents

Introduction... 1

Part I - My View of God 5

Chapter 1: Father Figure 7

Chapter 2: Perception Impacts Engagement 11

Chapter 3: Feelings and Truth 15

Chapter 4: Be. Loved.. 17

Chapter 5: More Than Savior 21

Chapter 6: Lucency 25

Part II - My View of Relationships 29

Chapter 7: Exploring Relationships 31

Chapter 8: Poor Stewardship 35

Chapter 9: The Value of Relationships... 39

Chapter 10: Purpose of Relationships... 41

Chapter 11: People Are Worth It.. 43

Chapter 12: Lower Your Expectations 47

Chapter 13: Reconciliation... 51

Part III - My View of Leaderhsip.. 55

Chapter 14: Leadership is Influence 57

Chapter 15: The Misconceptions of Leadership... 63

Chapter 16: Branches of Leadership 71

Chapter 17: Compound Influence 75

Part IV - My View of Success 77

Chapter 18: The Value of a Journey.. 79

Chapter 19: Pliable Structure 83

Chapter 20: Circumstantial Slavery 85

Chapter 21: Challenges: Opportunities or Excuses.. 89

Chapter 22: Big Picture.. 91

INTRODUCTION

"The one who states his case first seems right, until the other comes and examines him." (Proverbs 18:17 ESV)

It is estimated that more than one million English words are currently in use. Although the average English speaker may know about forty thousand words, they only actively use about twenty thousand of them. Words are the expressions of life, the architects of reality, and the influencers of destiny. Words have power and given time and context, can hold significant influence.

The word "perspective" has affected my life the most. As I stated earlier, words are an expression of life. To clarify, the word "perspective" did not make the impact. Instead, the way in which the word applied to certain circumstances, situations, and ideas has shifted the course of my life.

The passage at the start of this book encapsulates the motivation and the purpose for writing it. I have embraced, then cross-examined, particular perspectives at various points in my life, which ultimately caused me to reconsider my point of view.

I have had the privilege to gain perspective about several subjects, but that would make for a lengthy book that I am not committed to writing at this time. However, there are a few key areas that I would like to identify within this book upon which perspective has had a profound impact: God, leadership, relationships, and success.

What Is Perspective?

Perspective shares the same characteristic as opinions since everybody has one. It is simply a point of view, the way we perceive and understand something, that ultimately affects our behavior and actions. There was a time when I considered it fashionable to wear an oversized Dickies' suit, creased with heavy starch, and Chuck Taylors. Then, I was introduced to J. Crew and embraced the fact that a pair of chinos, a gingham button-down shirt, and a merino wool sweater were more suitable choices. In general, I learned that form-fitting clothes were not a detriment to my masculinity.

Perspective is a vantage point that is exemplified in various ways. It can be illustrated in the multiple cameras set up on a football field to monitor a game or the eyewitnesses standing in different areas viewing the same situation. I am confident you can recall a time that your opinion was swayed due to another viewpoint. I know that I can. My perspective is constantly being challenged and changed. Now, this may be perceived as unstable. Still my goal is never to have my perspective succumb to one that is inferior to the previous view. If my perspective is changed, the succeeding one should be an improvement from its predecessor.

What Impact Does Perspective Have on Our Lives?

External forces frequently influence our perspective. There are some forces that we intimately trust, where our values have docked and cast anchor, whereas others are like a cool, passing wind that brushes up against our skin just long enough for us to reconsider our current attire. My decisions, my responses, my choices, and my actions are all a direct result or product of my perspective, the helm of the ship that steers my life in a particular direction.

There is a passage in the Bible that states "a little leaven leavens the whole lump" (Galatians 5:9 ESV). Leaven is a substance or agent, such as yeast, that is used to make the dough rise. The presence of this leavening agent impacts the entire lump of dough. In context, the passage refers to how a slight inclination of error, deception, or lie can permeate one's whole belief system. Our belief system affects our actions, so consider the outcomes derived from a belief system that has been compromised by deception. Consider the stereotypes, generalizations, oppression, hatred, and the long list of societal ills that plague humanity, that are generated by this "leaven" that we have introduced into the dough.

Most of the behavior that we find to be unacceptable originates from taught and reinforced ideas. What we value or devalue is a result of what we have been exposed to. During my professional career, I noticed a chasm that existed between our sales and operations teams. The operations team was frustrated by the sales team because they believed that they made unrealistic promises, which increased the pressure on them. The sales team would refer to the operations team as the "Sales Prevention Department" because of failures to fulfill commitments.

I realized that both sides accused the other of indifference when, in actuality, it was a matter of inexposure and being unaware of what the other team was going through. Neither team had truly been immersed in their counterparts' world. Therefore, assumptions were made without experience, which led to an inaccurate depiction of the other team. In the instances where members of either team had the opportunity to get exposed to an environment outside of the norm, there was a greater appreciation, level of understanding, and respect that each team member gained from the experience. Perspective offers the opportunity to reshape the reality that may have been constructed by ignorance.

Is There a Good and a Bad Perspective?

To answer the question of whether there is such a thing as a good and a bad perspective, the subject of the observation and the origin in which the perspective is being captured must be considered. Simply put, what are you looking at, and from where are you looking?

If the goal is to decipher a license plate, the view from the 22nd floor of a building may not provide the best results. However, if the goal is to get a look at the city's skyline, the view from the identical location may prove to be more successful. A good metric of whether a perspective is good or bad is in what is produced. If perspective impacts our decisions, responses, and actions, then we can deduce that the nature of the results and experiences reflects the nature of our perspective.

As you read this book, may the question, "What is my perspective producing?" resonate through your mind. What results are you seeing in life as opposed to what you want to see? Could the variance or disconnect be due to a perspective that needs adjusting?

We can be fearful of asking these types of questions because they foster accountability. There is a flawed sense of comfort that accompanies the inclination to redirect responsibility elsewhere. This provides temporary security and stifles growth. How much of our potential will fail to be realized because we refuse to face the possibility that we may not have been seeing things as clearly as we thought?

The goal of this book is to present a concept to you that has marked my life: the way to convince a crooked stick that it is crooked is simply placing it next to a straight stick. The expression is not meant to be self-righteous or condescending. The point is that I prefer to present an example for you to make a comparison and assess instead of making an assertion of a fallacy. So, if you are willing to travel and to engage beyond the book's introduction, I offer you the opportunity to gaze through the lens of my view, not necessarily to adopt my perspective, but so that you may reconsider your own.

PART I –
MY VIEW OF GOD

CHAPTER 1:
Father Figure

I grew up with two father figures in my life: my "stepped-up" father and my biological father. I grew up with the notion that my stepfather was my birth father, as I had no other reason to think otherwise. It wasn't until I reached my adolescent years that I started putting the pieces together to realize this was not the case. This led me to ask questions about my origin and my biological father, whom I met at the age of 14.

My stepfather, whose value is in no way lowered in my sight because we did not share the same bloodline, was a disciplinarian. He was a firm, strong-willed, seemingly fearless individual. At times I would catch glimpses suggesting that a softer side existed in his life.

One occasion, on Father's Day, my brother and I presented a robe to him, and he began to cry. At the time, I did not understand what it was about the robe that made him cry. I know now that it had nothing to do with the robe itself. I will come back to that later.

I feared my stepfather growing up. I feared the consequences and repercussions that were subsequent to my disobedience or lying: the catalyst for most of the trouble that I experienced. Like most children, I didn't accept responsibility for my actions; I focused on the associated consequences and judged the punishment to be disproportionate to the crime.

My stepfather had no problem physically disciplining me. My young and immature perception of him was that he was cruel, harsh, and unfair. For years, this perception created a relational wedge between us. With the growing questions about my origin, the result was an apathetic relationship that simply consisted of walking on eggshells and maneuvering through the existing maze of unspoken and unresolved tension.

I met my biological father in my early teenage years. He and my mother separated when I was very young, and she never spoke about him in a positive or negative manner. I'm thankful for this because I neither had expectations nor resentment for him. Before we met, I had no pre-conceived notion, just curiosity. Would he look like me? How would he respond to me? You know, the basic questions.

The development of our new relationship was interesting. So many of the foundational years had been spent apart that I don't believe either one of us saw any value in trying to redeem that time. When I met him, it was just like meeting a stranger. We both seemed to want to start from the point that we were at. He didn't try to be this parental figure. It seemed like he didn't want to be overbearing and only wanted to be a friend. We didn't live close to one another, so we had a long-distance relationship for many years. We stayed in contact from that point, but our relationship was very surface level. The roots of our relationship were stable and secure, just not very deep.

So why am I telling you about my childhood and relationship with my two fathers? I'm glad you asked. So as Calhoun Tubbs would say, "I wrote a song about it. Like to hear it? Here it go!"[1] I didn't actually write a song, and you should be thankful for that, but I will explain. There is one more factor that I must mention before I delve into the reason why I detailed my relationship with my dads.

Origins

My introduction to God was subtle and progressive. My family didn't attend church and we had minimal to no discussion about God, so my reference point was faint and obscure, at best. The occasional Christian infomercial, the handful of visits to a friend's church, and the movies *Bill and Ted's Bogus Journey* and *Clash of the Titans* were the extent of examples I

---

1 *In Living Color*

could draw from when referencing God. We'll just say that I had a peculiar perspective of who God is.

Later in life, when I decided to enter into a personal relationship with God, the perception of my two fathers played a significant role in my perception of God. As I stated earlier, I saw my stepfather as a disciplinarian, harsh and firm with glimpses of a soft side if I caught him at the right time. Due to the circumstances, I saw my biological father as a distant friend who maintained an amiable, but shallow relationship. These are the characteristics that I associated with a father. So, when the concept that God is our Heavenly Father was introduced to me, it was these former perceptions that I began to project upon Him. To me, He was this distant, firm, occasionally friendly disciplinarian whom I needed to acknowledge, but rarely engage.

CHAPTER 2:
Perception Impacts Engagement

How we see or perceive God will determine or impact how we engage with Him. It impacts how we respond to the information that we obtain about Him. It also impacts how we communicate, which ultimately affects how our reality is formed.

I have noticed a common tendency within the ranks of humankind that definitely shapes our outlook. We are inclined to project the ideologies, encounters, and perspectives that we have been exposed to amongst our fellow man onto our Heavenly Father. We tend to view Him through life's kaleidoscope that produces a very abstract and eclectic representation. We apply the filter of our finite human experience onto the canvas of an infinite subject, resulting in a less than desirable expression.

I have also observed that people would much rather refer or speak to the universe than God.

I have a theory for the cause of this redirected dialogue. The word "God" has often been associated with limitations, parameters, regulations, religion, and legalism. There have been negative connotations affiliated with God, largely due to what has been displayed by those who have claimed to represent Him, and the information conveyed about Him.

These perceptions have caused masses to distance themselves from the concept of a divine personhood, especially one that has established standards which we are instructed to adhere to. However, the universe is often characterized by vastness and portrayed as the epitome of uninhibited freedom. No limitations and no box to place it in, and people like the idea of not being restricted. I can understand the appeal to lean towards the latter based on this information, but what if the lens through which God is being viewed is distorted or simply in need of a good cleaning?

You See?…Therefore You Act

There was an occasion that Jesus asked His disciples, "Who do you say that I am?" (Matthew 16:15). He wanted to know or rather He wanted them to be aware and address their perception of who He was. I was listening to "Salvation," a song originated by Goapele. I enjoy her music and ethereal voice. As the song played, I was captivated by a lyric that caused my mind to ponder for a while. Her lyrics were asking an unknown God to reveal Himself.

Now, I am unaware of Goapele's spiritual proclivities, and that is not actually the subject of this conversation. However, I am certain that many can relate to the sentiment behind her statement. I can understand the sense of futility that comes with trying to communicate with someone whom you really know nothing about, yet making the attempt because you are in search of answers. The truth is that you cannot operate beyond the revelation or perception that you possess or embrace.

Have you ever been given information about someone before you met them, whether good, bad, accurate, or inaccurate? That information became the barometer of how you treated them. For example, let's say that I was given an opportunity to take on a new role within my company, and I was told that there was an individual within the group that I would oversee who was extremely difficult to work with. They are the "glass is half empty" type of individual. They have a gift of finding what's wrong in what's right. They are contentious, overly opinionated, and they tend to major in the minor.

Should I choose to take this information at face value, my encounter with this person will probably be tense and guarded. I will probably approach this person with a battle-ready attitude. I would want to quickly establish that there is no tolerance for discord and an attitude adjustment would be required. Every sentiment and action just listed would be based on the information that I was given and the perception that was forged from that information.

Whether or not the information was accurate is immaterial. What is relevant is that my perception of this individual impacted how I approached them and ultimately shaped the encounter that I had with them. Everything associated with this person is filtered through my perception of them; therefore, it affects how I interpret what they say, how I assess the motivation behind their actions, and even how I perceive their perception of me.

The factors that influenced my perception of God helped construct the box that I placed Him in. It is not my intention to sound haughty or blasphemous in making the statement of placing God in a box, but rather conveying how my misconceptions created limits for the One who is limitless, thus limiting my experience with Him.

I learned that God does not impose or force Himself onto people. He invites and accepts invitations into fellowship, but He doesn't "crash the party." Jesus says, "Behold I **stand** at the door and knock" (Revelation 3:20 ESV). He has full power and ability to walk in, yet He stands and knocks, denoting the respect that He has for the reception.

CHAPTER 3:
Feelings and Truth

In Psalm 31:22 (TPT), the writer proclaims, "I spoke hastily when I said, 'The Lord has deserted me.'" You have heard the admonition that you should think before you speak, right? The truth of the matter is that you always think before you speak because your tongue does not operate independent of your brain. A more accurate statement is that you spoke before you fully considered.

Frequently, we allow our emotions to override our good judgment or the truth that we have in the repository of our minds. Our feelings can disguise themselves as truth and distort our view of the Lord. Sometimes we experience feelings that are contrary to truth, and what we choose to embrace will impact the quality of our life.

Faulty Gauge

Our feelings are not always an accurate representation of what truth is. Our emotions are healthy when they express, reflect, or are driven by truth. When we allow the emotions to dictate truth in our minds, that is when they become disruptive and no longer credible.

If our emotions were a car component, they would serve in the role as an indicator or signal, not the steering wheel. Our emotions, our feelings are response signals. In the stock market, they would be considered lagging indicators, telling the tale of what has already happened. There was an event that took place that triggered a specific emotion. So, the emotion can be used as a point of reference to determine the cause. This can be beneficial because in identifying the cause, we can then determine what the response should be.

The problem is when we allow the signaling mechanism to assume a navigational role in our lives. Emotions and feelings were never intended to validate truth. They can point us back to their inception so that we look at the truth in that situation, but they should never be the barometer by which truth is substantiated.

Consider the following statement and the thought process that is associated with it: "I feel lonely: therefore, that must mean that I am alone, and I have been deserted." This is what the psalmist recognized. He allowed his emotions to be the validator of truth, and the result was that he spoke in haste and that which he spoke was a fallacy.

Did he feel like the Lord deserted him? Yes. Did the Lord really desert him? No. The circumstance was the catalyst for the emotion, and rather than looking at the circumstance through the lens of God's character, he looked at it through the lens of his emotions. Peering through that lens gave him the illusion that God had deserted him. The Lord never deserts us, and our emotions do not have the grounds to substantiate that claim.

CHAPTER 4:
Be. Loved.

I mentioned earlier that when my brother and I were younger, we presented a robe to our dad, and he began to cry. It didn't make sense to me at the time why he was crying, and in all honesty, it seemed a little awkward and uncomfortable. To me, it was just a robe, but to him, it was about the acknowledgement. The gift was recognition of his role as a father to us. This is what he valued.

Faith is what pleases God. Being fully persuaded and convinced of who He is. Faith is the response to a correct perspective of who He is, and this is what brings Him delight. This is the "robe" or the gift that we present that pleases Him.

I believe that the Lord views His role, as Father to us, to be a privilege. I have encountered many people that consider themselves to be a burden to the Lord. It comes out in their speech. "I just don't see how God could love someone like me." We view ourselves as burdens while He describes us as His beloved. Beloved means to be dearly loved, highly valued, and precious. As we see God for the Father that He is, one that us holds dear and highly esteems us as His children, His offspring, we then start to become the reflection of this perspective. Simply put, our interpretation of His opinion about us impacts how we view ourselves.

We have or I have had this notion that prior to Jesus, God just cringed at the sight of us because of our sin, but looking at Jesus' life, that is not the sentiment that is revealed. He didn't cringe at the woman who was caught in the very act of adultery. He didn't criticize the tax collector who greedily took advantage of his own people, employed by their oppressors, for selfish gain. He didn't condemn those who betrayed Him, that previously declared undying devotion to Him. He embraced them, showed them their value, and gave His life for them.

Jesus is the express will and image of the invisible God. There has been such a misconception about who our Father is that the depictions rendered of Him resemble that of a tyrannical, frigid, vindictive, and intangible being that sadistically plays a game of Russian roulette with the fate of humanity. That can be no further from the truth than the east is from the west.

A Dim View

In one of my favorite stories, a father's nature was ill perceived by two of his sons. One of his sons, after becoming rebellious and wayward, came to his senses and decided that it would be expedient to return home to his father's household. This was after he demanded to receive his portion of the inheritance and then wasted it on superfluous spending and indulgence. He considered his actions to be too great of a transgression against his father to expect reconciliation in the form of sonship, so he resigned to seek admission in the position of a servant.

He assumed that his father would begrudge him since the family name was dishonored and the wealth that was accumulated as an inheritance was squandered. He considered the shame, most likely brought upon his father, that succeeded his poor decisions and couldn't fathom that his father would respond in any other way, but to reciprocate the same. An eye for an eye, right?

As he cautiously drew near, he was in utter disbelief and shock to witness his father enthusiastically approaching, arms open wide ready to embrace him. He was not only welcomed back but found himself reinstated to the same position that he held prior to his departure: a son and legal heir of his father. I would like to note that this idea of reinstatement was one that only took up residence in the son's mind. Can you imagine the cyclone of emotions and thoughts whirling within him? In addition to this, the father also called for a celebration to commemorate the return of his son.

While this appeared to be a joyous occasion, it was not accepted by all as such. The eldest son did not share in the rhapsody. Upon hearing about the celebration that was taking place, he refused to participate. He was embittered and had to be sought out by the father himself to find out what the problem was. He laid out his indictment against his father.

He asserted that even though he had worked on his father's estate and in his business for years without any disloyalty, his father never once gave him recognition for his commitment. The offense due to the lack of acknowledgement was multiplied when the younger son returned from his debauchery and was celebrated. The older son resented the perceived inequity demonstrated by his father's actions.

I can imagine that there had to be a level of grief besieging the heart of this father as he realized that both of his sons had an incorrect view of him and how he felt about them both. Not only did the younger son think that he would be vindictive, but he also assumed that his sonship was contingent upon his actions instead of his connection. The older son viewed his father as an indifferent, dismissive taskmaster who was partial and unfair. Both views were contradicted in the father's responses, respectively.

To the younger son, the father's true sentiments were seen through his response at his return. To the older son, after the indictment, the father responded, "Son, you are always with me, and all that is mine is yours" (Luke 15:31 NIV). What he was expressing was that his loyalty did not go unnoticed or unappreciated, and the access to his entire estate has always been and always will be in his grasp. His love did not have to be earned by either of his sons. In the same way, I can imagine that our Heavenly Father longs for us to see Him in the proper light that we may recognize we have always been the apple of His eye, not objects of scorn.

Choice of View

Like most people, I have not been spared my portion of problems and tragedy. I have experienced an identity crisis, a court-ordered leave of absence from the freedom of civil society, and the loss of several loved ones, to name a few. In every one of those instances, I faced the temptation of defining God through those circumstances, meaning that I was faced with the temptation of allowing the nature of the circumstance to represent or reflect the nature of God. The now obvious danger lies within this verity: should the circumstances prove to be adverse, unbecoming, and surmounting, my view of God becomes less and less appealing. I find myself questioning.

Now, let me parenthetically insert here that there is a difference between asking questions and questioning. We ask questions to discover, to bring understanding where there is a void. I believe that questioning derives from a posture of doubt that is not interested in understanding but is rooted in accusation.

To illustrate this point, in the Book of Genesis, a question was proposed to the female representative of humanity, Eve, that was not intended to gain understanding and insight, but to produce doubt. The question was, "Did God really say…?" In every circumstance, we get to decide how we are going to look at God, through the situation or through His Word.

If we choose the circumstance, then we ask questions such as, "If God is good, then why…?" or "Would a loving God really allow…?" We have been hurt and wounded and are now responding out of that place of pain. If we choose His Word, then our springboard is that His nature is good and is not a variable; it is unchanging. Therefore, the circumstance provides the opportunity or becomes the platform in which His nature can be displayed as it triumphs over adversity.

We are admonished in the Scriptures that "without faith, it is impossible to please Him" (Hebrews 11:6 NIV). To piggyback on that statement, it is impossible to have faith without a proper perception of God and a knowledge of His will. Faith is being fully persuaded and convinced. While it is often misconstrued or erroneously defined as an unwarranted expectation void of any substance, on the contrary, it is actually the response to a substantiated and proven claim. God's word, His laws, and principles are true and established; therefore, my faith is a product of my understanding of this.

CHAPTER 5:
More Than Savior

One of the more difficult, yet most impactful, shifts of perspective that I have acquired is my view of Jesus as Lord and King, not just Savior. The phrase "Jesus is Lord" is entrenched within Christian vernacular; however, I'm afraid that the gravity of the statement has been disproportionate to its common use. This is apparent, especially in the Western culture that has become estranged from the concepts of kings and kingdoms. The United States is actually the very product of rebellion from this type of system or government, so any relation to it seems very foreign.

I have come to find that no matter how displaced I may be from this concept, it is absolutely essential for me to grasp if I intend to live out the purpose that I was created for. Seeing Jesus as King and Lord is the springboard from which my life is catapulted. It affects how I manage my finances, how I parent, the quality of my marriage, the way I perform my job, and the way I interact with people. How so? The answer is found in the nature of a king and how a king relates to his kingdom and the citizens.

Save Me, Don't Rule Me

My experience is that I recognized and fully accepted that Jesus was Savior, but I did not as willingly accept Him as King. Accepting Him as Savior was easy. I recognized that I was in need. There was a danger that I was facing that required intervention, assistance, and rescue.

Although it still required humility to admit that I needed help, ultimately, it was easy to accept that it would be to my benefit. Who wouldn't embrace that which is going to benefit themselves, right? This is why I said "accepting Him as Savior was easy" in comparison to accepting Him as King.

Now you may ask, "Why was that such a big deal?" Glad you asked. It becomes a bigger deal once you realize what a king is and what that means for you. So, let's take a moment to delve into or define what a king is.

A king is defined as "one who reigns, who possesses and exercises sovereign power and complete rule." A king is completely autonomous in his government and is not required to justify any decision that is made, any action that is taken, or seek the counsel of anyone outside of himself... [pause for effect.] I can almost see some who are reading this beginning to squirm as they read those ... few statements.

Why is that? Probably the same reason that it caused me to be reluctant. It meant that someone was in charge of my life and had more say-so about my life than I did. That makes things very uncomfortable, especially for a people that have been so indoctrinated in the idea of independence. Words such as "submission" become an expletive in our vocabulary and our resistance heightens in the very introduction of the concept.

Alignment

A king influences everything in his kingdom: the culture, the values, the attire, the economy, the food, the language, the financial structure, and the arts. A king's territory or domain is a direct expression or reflection of the king, no different than your home is an expression of you. Since the king sets the standard, that means, should I desire to be a citizen of that kingdom, I am giving up my right to live independent of that standard.

I have given up my right to my own opinion. His opinion is my opinion on any matter. My preferences are aligned with the King's preferences. He is the landlord, owner, and has the right to everything within His domain.

As challenging as this may be to read at this time, it is necessary to establish because if it is not settled at the beginning, then our journey will be compared to building a house on sand instead of our foundation being laid on rock. When the "winds," that is, the challenges and oppositions that come in life appear, the house built on an unstable foundation will undoubtedly succumb and fall while the house built on a solid foundation will withstand the pressures and be found erect once the storms come to a cessation.

The endeavor or desire of a king is to expand his territory; the same is true for our King. To expand the reach of His influence beyond His current boundaries. This intention gives us purpose because He will send out a delegation in order to have this endeavor realized. We are that delegation; we are those ambassadors.

The benefit to embracing this perspective is realized when the majesty and the benefits of this Kingdom come into view: provision, double portion, more than enough, cancellation of debts, no more toil and sweat, restitution of what was lost, reinstatement of position, reaffirmation of purpose, love with no strings attached, peace that transcends understanding, joy inexpressible…just to name a few perks. Those who are faced with the obstacle of threading the proverbial camel through the eye of a needle and choose to relinquish the cargo of independence from God will find that they are the intended beneficiaries of this ever-expanding Kingdom. The question will be if you think the value of the offer is worth the cost.

CHAPTER 6:
Lucency

Over the years, there have been activities and pastimes that have gained my interest and provided me with various levels of enjoyment. Chess, college football, and Marvel movies are my guilty pleasures. Now, I'm not in an active chess club nor do I have someone that I regularly play with, so my engagement is normally limited to the online chess platforms that are available.

College football generally lasts for a brief season and, depending on your allegiance, the brevity of the season can be more significant than others. I don't consider myself to be a fair-weather fan. I am quite loyal to my team, GO GATORS, by the way; however, my enthusiasm dwindles in between seasons. I am not the fanatic that is constantly keeping up with statistics on players and can recite the obscure play that led to a third down conversion 15 years ago.

As the Marvel Cinematic Universe expands and seems to monopolize Hollywood cinema, my interest peaks and wanes when new characters are introduced, but again it is simply a pastime that I engage in. Where am I going with this, you ask? Humanity is not God's hobby.

We are not an activity that God leisurely addresses when He finds the time. Humanity is actually God's largest investment. He placed everything in this investment because He gave Himself for the purpose of yielding a great return. He holds us at such great value, knowing our potential because as the Supreme Architect and Creator, He is aware of what can be accomplished through us.

Unto Something

What is all this leading to? To what end? What purpose? Why is clarity concerning God so important? The answer is that without clarity of who He is, then it is unclear who I really am and the reason for my existence. I lack clarity of purpose.

Purpose is determined by the manufacturer of the product, not the product itself. Without the awareness of purpose, the fulfillment of purpose cannot be achieved. This is why seeking God's guidance and instruction is so essential. He knows our intended purpose, and His instruction provides us with guidance in how to accomplish that purpose. It is also confirmation of success because He has promised that "Every place that the sole of your foot will tread upon I have given you…" (Joshua 1:3 ESV). If this is true, then that means, as He orders or directs my steps, I can have confidence that I have authority in the area in which He is leading me to go.

There is this characteristic or quality of partnership that the Lord has emphasized in our relationship with Him. This partnership is necessary in His objective being accomplished on this earth. I have a canvas hanging in my office, with a quote that He gave me, derived from Matthew 18:18. It says, "Without God, man cannot. Without man, God will not." What this statement is implying is that God is committed to His will being performed on this earth through the agent that He commissioned, humanity…us.

This is not something that we can do on our own; rather, we rely on this partnership to help us fulfill it. Jesus says that "…apart from Me you can do nothing" (John 15:5). Whether we acknowledge it or not, without Jesus' life-breathing presence and activity in our lives, we cannot operate, function, or even exist. He holds the fabric of life together. "The God who made the world and everything in it, being Lord of Heaven and earth, does not live in temples made by man, nor is He served by human hands, as though He needed anything, since He Himself gives to all mankind life and breath and everything" (Acts 17:24-25).

Acknowledging that I cannot do anything apart from the Lord is not low self-esteem or catering to the ego of a self-absorbed being, but it is a reminder that I should never be separated from my Source. For me, to try to do anything without God is to believe that I can separate myself from the whole and still be whole. It would be like losing one of my appendages and still considering myself complete. I am not! I am missing an important part that helps my body function at the capacity that it was designed to.

Replica

My desire is to love as the Father loves. To live a life that creates a legacy of kindness and honors the Lord. I never want my view of Him to be cavalier or familiar, in the sense that I lose awareness of how great He really is.

There is a psalm that speaks of the "beauty of holiness" (Psalm 29:2). Holiness refers more to the state of something rather than an action. Holiness is sacredness, apartness. Something is considered sacred due to its uniqueness. It is one of a kind, and its value cannot be measured. There is nothing to compare it to.

"Who is like the Lord?" asked the writer of a psalm. He exists outside of time. He is the beginning as we relate to time. Everything started from Him as He is the Source of all things. All that has been created has His fingerprint on it, and it is by His creativity that the complexities of humanity and the universe were formed. It is the Creator, not the creation, that should be venerated.

When I am aware of the Lord's greatness, it empowers me because it is He on whom I am relying to supply my strength, wisdom, resources, and power. It is in this soil of understanding that my roots are established, producing a life destined to leave a mark in this world.

PART II –
MY VIEW OF RELATIONSHIPS

CHAPTER 7:
Exploring Relationships

When you think of the word "relationship," what is the first thing that pops into your mind? Romance? Family? Marriage? Friends? All of these concepts can be enveloped in the term, but simply put, a relationship is a connection. There exists a link that joins together, and this link can be strengthened, weakened, bonded, or severed. It can take on various applications, as noted earlier; however, I am of the persuasion that the purpose is universal. While it is not my intention to string you along or delay to cause you to continue reading, I do believe that it is essential to discuss a few key areas that will provide more substance to what I believe is the purpose of relationships. Should you choose to endure, I think that it will be beneficial to you.

Over the course of time and observation, I have encountered several reasons people have chosen to be married or to get into relationships. For the most part, none of those reasons are congruent with the one that, I believe, is paramount. Before I divulge my proposition of why relationships are vital, let's take a look at some of the common reasons that people enter into relationships.

Companionship (Looking to Be Loved)

I don't think that it is too far-fetched or too general a statement to say that everyone wants to be loved. Parenthetically, I have to add that everyone wants to be loved in the manner or to the extent they understand love. Some see love as a "second-hand emotion" or feeling.

To some, love is a concept that cannot be described, only experienced, and its intangibility doesn't negate its existence, it just transcends the sensual realm in which we would try to contain it. My point here is that no matter how you define love, everyone longs for it. The caveat is that your perception of love affects your expectation, especially for the one whom you are relying on to give it to you.

Love is the response of seeing the value and worth of someone. It is the byproduct of seeing people how God sees people. When that perspective is embraced, the response is kindness, patience, edification, forgiveness, sincerity, and the like. When it is realized that this value has been attributed to you already and incessantly poured over you, then the dependence on receiving this love from someone else goes away, liberating and empowering you to exemplify this to others with no strings attached.

Provisional (Looking for Security)

Although this is not a reason that I believe most people would readily admit, it is nonetheless a motivation for being in a relationship. No one wants to be thought of as being a gold-digger, which is a surface-level categorization. At a deeper level, I believe that the motive is truly security. The relationship is beneficial because it offers something that is lacking. It is the answer to the question "Who is going to take care of me?"

We are enveloped in a system where we are constantly seeking provision. We work for and look for means of provision, finding ourselves completely preoccupied with survival. Thus, we have identified being in a relationship, as a means to facilitate these facets of provision and survival. It is a cumbersome and laborious effort that we were not intended to bear. We have fended for ourselves because we were taught that this is the only way, but it gets tiring, and we search for rest.

"Fear not, little flock, for it is your Father's good pleasure to give you the Kingdom" (Luke 12:32). It is the intention of our Father in Heaven to give us access to His entire estate. To partake in all that belongs to Him. It is in this knowledge that we shed our orphan clothes and exchange them with royal garb, coming to a realization that we have a benefactor whose desire is to take care of us fully.

Acceptance (Looking for Significance)

There is a hope that within a relationship, one's value is authenticated based on how they are treated. This is really akin to the aforementioned motivation for companionship. We want to be welcomed in, to feel like we are a part of something.

I spent a good percentage of my life seeking to be accepted, to be welcomed in. I can't say that I was denied treatment that would imply that I wasn't; nevertheless, I continuously pursued it. In retrospect, I realize that I so vehemently sought it out because I hadn't yet accepted that I was already approved of. I was already good enough, and I didn't have to perform to validate that.

I wasted a lot of time trying to convince others of a facade, of a persona that I so desperately wanted to encapsulate to feel like I was significant. I lied to maintain the integrity of this fictional character that I was portraying. The inconsistencies were spotted by a few, but I worked hard to avoid those who could see through the role. For those whom I was able to beguile, I reveled in the intoxicating feeling of importance that they would attribute to me.

Vanity of vanities. It was insatiable and unsustainable. It was like putting new wine into old wineskins. It would only be a matter of time before my insufficient container for this affirmation would leak out and I would seek to be filled again.

Our true significance can be found within the exchange at the Skull of Golgotha. No, this is not a realm in the Lord of the Rings. It is where Jesus the Christ exchanged His life in a display of the valuation that He held ours in. It wasn't an act to show how wretched we were, but to show how significant we are. There is not an instrument of measure that could quantify God's love for us.

Notwithstanding, the magnitude and enormity of His sacrifice gives indication of the value that He has ascribed to us. Would you ever pay $200,000 for a $10,000 car? Of course not! It's not worth it. So, riddle me this, if your life wasn't worth it, then why would God pay such a high price to offer His Son as a ransom for reconciliation?

Obligation (Looking to Pay a Debt)

Now, I know that this may seem a little abstract and even outlandish, but, given some consideration, I believe that I can make my case. Some people enter into relationships because they feel like they have to. It may be because the other party has invested time and resources, so they now feel like they owe them to be in the relationship. Or, perhaps, there are expectations from third parties that place pressure due to maintaining status or reputation.

The glaring problem with this motivation is the lack of sincerity. No one really benefits from the relationship. Obligation will turn a relationship into a desert if it is not coupled with the wellspring of joy that is only present when it is viewed as a gift not a debt. I am joyfully committed to my wife, so my obligation to her is not a burden to me, it is a privilege.

Duty, in the context of a relationship, can be a fine line to walk separating a healthy, thriving relationship from a feeble, deteriorating one. When paying back a debt, the focus is not on adding value, it is on eliminating the liability. It is about coming out from under something that is weighing you down. If this is the motivating force behind being in a relationship, how long…correction…how fruitful can that relationship be?

Length of time does not necessarily equate to a healthy relationship. I have seen examples of high-tenure, low-quality relationships held together only by familiarity and fear rather than love and devotion. Simply going through the motions should not be the accepted norm.

CHAPTER 8:
Poor Stewardship

Have you ever seen or purchased an item and there was a sign that stated "Handle with care" on it? Why was that message necessary? It is because the improper handling of the item could result in damage.

There are two areas that I would like to discuss that I believe can be a detriment to relationships: inconvenience and distractions. A perception of inconvenience can lead to a casual stewarding of relationships with God and people. It can cause us to downplay or even dismiss the importance and impact of engaging in the relationship.

Inconvenience can serve as an agent or catalyst for developing relationships or as the wedge that only cultivates and reinforces selfishness. I can recall being invited by a coworker to take a trip to participate in a meeting that I did not honestly believe would be pertinent to me. He thought that it would be beneficial to me because there were some key figures from our company that were going to be there. He thought that it would be advantageous for me to meet and become acquainted with them, especially because my ambition was to build my career with this company.

I tend to seize opportunities to meet new people because I know that relationships can be leveraged. I know that sounds manipulative, but I say that with the understanding that this world revolves around relationships and the quality of your life is largely determined by how well you manage them. There is an African proverb that states, "If you want to go fast, go alone. If you want to go far, go together." Back to the story.

As I agreed to go, my coworker also suggested that we ride to the meeting together and we could also share a room to cut down on expenses. While this was logical, I found myself reluctant to go because, in all honesty, I wanted my privacy. I enjoyed the option of riding in my car and listening to the podcasts and music that I chose or simply riding in silence. I knew that if we rode together, it would be hours that we were sitting in the car, and, at some point in time and possibly not the time that I chose, I would be obligated to engage in conversation.

Then there was the inconvenience of having to share a hotel room. I know, first-world problems. Although it came close, I did not allow these immature sentiments to deter me. The day came for the trip, and as I anticipated, I was forced to engage in conversation, which ended up being insightful and meaningful. I learned some important things about him and his life on that day and should I have succumbed to the selfishness that was trying to arise, I would have missed out on the enriched discussions that we had.

I would have missed the opportunity to participate in the very thing that I so adamantly advocate, which is building relationships, all because of a moment of perceived inconvenience. If handled properly, inconvenience can be forged into an opportunity to gain insight and bring value.

Are You Paying Attention?

Another case of poor relational stewardship is found in distractions. Distraction can be a thorn to relationships. It is a deterrent that can inflict so much discomfort that it prevents the relationship from growing closer and stifles engagement. Engagement is the currency of relationships. It is what makes the relationship worthwhile and valuable, but it takes being actively present.

When I speak of "being actively present," I am not only referring to existing in the moment, but also being attentive in the moment. It is commonplace in this age to go out to a restaurant and see a couple or a family sitting at a table together, but everyone is on their phone. Everyone is physically present, but they are hardly aware of the other individuals within their vicinity. I am not bashing technology here, but simply using it as a baseline to identify a common enemy: distraction.

Distraction is defined as anything that prevents someone from giving their full attention to something else. Failure to commit our full attention normally results in mishaps of some kind or gradual deterioration. It is like pulling on a loose thread on a garment; over time the fabric begins to unravel until there is a gaping hole that is visible and the first question that is asked is "How did that happen?"

I suggest that it happened in progressive, consistent stages. It spreads into different areas of life, and the only remedy is intentional refusal. It will require that the opportunity for distractions to have a leading role is declined or rescinded.

This may mean that your phone is silenced or left in another room during dinner. Or it may mean choosing not to multitask, which I believe is a myth anyway, but that is for another time. Ok, quick sidebar, but it is relevant to this conversation. Don't confuse the ability to do more than one thing at a time with the ability to focus on more than one thing at a time. You will only be able to give your full, 100% attention to one thing at a time. So, give your attention to what matters most when it matters most.

CHAPTER 9:
The Value of Relationships

In the past, I have taken my various relationships for granted due to my lack of awareness of their value. You give your time and resources to that which you perceive has value. Value, like beauty, is in the eye of the beholder, which gives credence to such adages like "One man's trash is another man's treasure."

The value of something is determined by what it can produce or provide. Think about it, if I make a purchase of a piece of clothing, I am exchanging the cost of the item for the value that I believe it will convey. Whether the value is in the fact that it will fill a hole in my wardrobe, replace a worn or torn item, solicit attention, etc., there is something that is being offered or provided that validates my purchase.

Proverbs 27:10 speaks of the value of stewarding and maintaining relationships and the benefit that it has. "Do not forsake your friend and your father's friend, and do not go to your brother's house in the day of your calamity. Better is a neighbor who is near than a brother who is far away." The point is that nurturing relationships can serve to be a great deal of help in times of need. What consolation to know that because of the relationships that you have established, you have a network of people around you that you can rely on when there is a need. The alternative is that, due to your mismanagement of your relationships, there are limited people to reach out to because there have been no investments made into them.

This is not an exclusive benefit to relationships, but it is one that is worth noting. I am also not suggesting that you simply get into relationships to meet your needs. Relationships are the cornerstones of community, and without them, instability is the result.

What's Changed?

A key to a thriving relationship is to not grow so familiar that you fail to appreciate the worth of the other. During my relatively short time being alive, I have been a part of several types of relationships. One of the most meaningful relationships that I have been blessed and fortunate enough to partake in is that of my marriage to my lovely wife, Destini. We have been married for 15 years, which have seemed to have just accelerated. In those 15 years, we have had disagreements, but have never fought. (I hate the fact that statement can be viewed as a deviation from the norm).

We have had our challenges that we had to overcome together, but our marriage itself was not the challenge, it was the external circumstance. Never have we second guessed our decision to commit our respective lives to the other. I trust my wife wholly, and, with her consent, I can say that her sentiments are the same for me. I think that the best way to summarize our marriage is pursuing convergence. We found that our pursuit has been not only to walk in the same direction, but also to get to the point that we are walking together as one instead of independent of one another.

This has been a consistent theme in our marriage. We have endearingly coined it as the "urge to merge." It was essential that we continuously aspired to get to know one another, understanding that our perspectives would adjust with time and experience. Development is a part of the human experience, and if we are not aware that this is taking place, we can find ourselves misinformed, thinking that we are current, when we are actually associating with a relic in our mind. Still engaging with the person we once knew or was previously familiar with, unaware that person has morphed into a new revision of themselves.

CHAPTER 10:
Purpose of Relationships

So then, I would like to propose that the main reason we enter into relationships is to partner in a commitment to fulfilling purpose. I think that it is often misinterpreted that Eve's purpose was to settle the problem of Adam's loneliness in the Garden of Eden. I believe that Adam, representing humanity, was charged to accomplish a task that, by himself, he was not able to do and needed a partner to fulfill something that was much greater than both of them.

We live in such a self-centered world system that we become preoccupied only with the things that promote and elevate ourselves. It is a foreign concept to consider that our lives are not our own and actually play a role in the fulfillment of something that may not necessarily have to do with just us. Of those who have made a commitment to acknowledge Jesus as Lord, we are often identified by the designation of the Body of Christ.

This is significant because a physical body is made up of many different parts, serving many different roles. Each part or member has a specific and unique purpose or functionality. However, each of these unique and significant roles and functionalities all serve to ensure that the body as a whole can operate to its created potential. Without these individuals, the body cannot accomplish the purpose that it was created for, thus affecting the environment and reality surrounding it.

I want to use this example, acknowledging that I am in no way an aficionado in the automotive realm, so all my car enthusiasts, be patient and have mercy on me. A gearbox is used in power transmission from the engine, through the clutch, to the wheels of the vehicle. It provides for the controlled application of power and torque using gears and gear trains. The car would not be able to start off from a standstill or climb inclines without a gear box. The vehicle would simply stall.

That gearbox was manufactured for a unique purpose, and that purpose could not be fulfilled independent from the application to the engine. Nor could that engine be able to fulfill its purpose without the application and presence of the gearbox. They are interdependent.

It is both humbling and honoring to understand that we are created to enrich the lives of others, and without each other, our lives are not enriched. When viewed from this perspective, it emphasizes the gravity of these connections, realizing that our need for one another is not a matter of filling a void or satisfying emotional destitution, but it is to catapult and aid in the consummation of our purpose.

CHAPTER 11:
People Are Worth It

People are worth it. Many would disagree; however, "Love believes all things, looking for the best in each one" (I Cor. 13:7 AMP). It is overwhelming to see how low people think of each other. There is a resounding cynicism and indifference towards our fellow humans that fills the mental chambers of society. We devour each other with our cannibalizing words that convey the message that we have no value.

It seems that we have adopted and embraced Agent Smith's perspective that humanity is a virus, and its only function is to spread its DNA by infecting and corrupting its host, ultimately causing dysfunction and disorder. Agent Smith was the main antagonist in the film *The Matrix*, in case you were wondering. This deceptive and destructive concept initiates a vicious cycle. One that produces a callousness of heart, which enables us to do unthinkable things to one another, which is witnessed and then undergirds the idea that people are not worth it.

Where is this concept coming from? What is its genesis? Normally, it is hurt or offense. Play this scenario out: someone is mistreated and over time begins to dislike people. Their hearts become hardened because of how they have been treated by people: therefore, the value they place on people starts to diminish. It is easy to throw away something that you don't value. They commit an atrocious crime. This crime is viewed by the masses, who are left in disgust. This case is generalized and now a perception grows, resuming the cycle. It must be broken. People are worth it!

What Is "It" All About?

What is the "it"? The "it" is the investment, the time, the patience. All because the "it" yields a return. The "it" that is offered has the potential to change lives and ultimately the world. In the culminating book of the Bible, the Lord's appearance was described to be as a jewel, arrayed in color and brilliance. This is significant as it creates an appreciation for people because we are made in His image and likeness. We are made in brilliance. Brilliance is defined as "intense brightness of light; vividness of color, exceptional talent or intelligence." The Lord is all of these definitions personified, and we are created out of this Source!

People are not their actions, although we tend to identify people by their actions. People are products of their chosen responses to life's situations. The cycle is broken by beginning to see people the way that God sees people. Seeing them for their created value and not their propensity to err.

Animal Attraction

Over the years, I have noticed a rise in what I consider to be an unhealthy transfer of affinity from people to animals. There are countless memes, merchandise, bumper stickers, etc., that denote this growing preference of animals over people. Although it may seem minute or harmless, there is a root that is deepening that is disturbing and needs to be addressed. That root is that people have been so offended and hurt by other people, that the value of people is diminishing in their sight. They would rather invest in something that cannot hurt them than someone who has the potential to hurt them.

Now, I am not against animals or animal lovers. I believe that their lives have value as well and should be treated with kindness because they are also God's creation. I do, however, believe that their worth should not supersede the life of a human being and should be placed in proper perspective.

Jesus, Himself, stated, "Look at the birds of the air: they neither sow nor reap nor gather into barns, and yet your heavenly Father feeds them. Are you not of more value than they?" (Matthew 6:26 ESV). Here, Jesus shows that He does see value in the animals, but He sees greater value in the ones that were created in His image. Due to the amassing hurt and offense, we have switched this and placed more value on animals than the ones who were created in His image. I reiterate, the cycle must be broken, and it starts with the simple concept: <u>PEOPLE ARE WORTH IT</u>!

CHAPTER 12:
Lower Your Expectations

There are standards, criterion, that impact the manner in which we operate in this life. These influence the places that we go to eat, the quality of clothes that we wear, the neighborhoods that we would ideally live in, the company that we work for or business we create, even the relationships that we are engaged in. Within that last statement is where we must exercise caution.

Most expectations are measured through comparing someone else to yourself. "You" become the barometer: therefore, meeting your expectations entails someone emulating you and the way that you do things. Some may feel that having expectations is not a negative thing, and the truth is that it depends on context. Where is it applied?

I have experienced that when I assign my expectations to the appointment of others, it often leads to being judgmental and critical. I will make statements such as, "If I were you…" or "If I was doing it…," etc. In those very statements, notice that "I" am the nucleus. "I" am the measuring stick which determines how something should be. The problem with this metric is that "I" am flawed. "I" occupy and take up residence in the most refining room on this earth, the room for improvement.

"You judge according to the flesh; I judge no one" (John 8:15). We are not to regard anyone in a manner apart from their created value, that is, the person that God intended for them to be. "From now on, therefore, we regard no one according to the flesh" (2 Corinthians 5:16).

I think that it is prudent to say that my expectations of a person should not exceed their commitment. What do I mean by that? The only grounds that I have to justify holding someone to a particular standard is if that person has conveyed that standard is one that they are committed to upholding. Otherwise, my standard or expectation is based on speculation or assumption.

Aspiration > Expectation

I had a young man who was working on my team, and, in my eyes, he had a lot of potential to excel in our company. The problem was that I could not motivate him to take initiative and go the extra mile. We were in a position where, due to our turnover, he ended up being one of the senior members on the team, and so my expectation was that he was going to take the reins and show himself to be a leader amongst those who had less tenure. Unfortunately, this was not the case. In fact, in some regard, he did even less than what was expected.

To my dismay and frustration, I found myself ready to write a scathing evaluation on him, and I was prepared to convey my disappointment to him during the review. Then I had an epiphany. This young man never committed to going the extra mile. He never committed to stepping up as a leader and being an example. These were my expectations that I projected on him, even though it came from a place of seeing his potential. It was at that point I realized that I could only hold him accountable for what he committed to, not what I wanted him to commit to.

I think that there is a difference between aspiration and expectation. I believe that Jesus had aspirations for his disciples, not expectations. He wanted the best for them; however, He didn't hold them to a standard in which they could not measure up. His corrections were calling them higher, to a place where they could live up to their potential, their created value.

The divergence of these two concepts takes place in the response. The response of aspiration is patience for the purpose of getting the person to the goal. The response of expectation is normally shame and condemnation for not reaching the goal. I think that we will find it liberating to free people from our expectations; at the same time, we will find it fulfilling to encourage people by our aspirations for them.

CHAPTER 13:
Reconciliation

Now since we have discussed the value and purpose of relationships, we come to the point where many of us have been challenged. What do we do with the relationships that have been damaged due to our failure to see their value and our mismanagement of them? Knowing that relationships are a key to the fulfillment of purpose, it would be expedient to consider the ones that have fallen by the wayside.

A hard pill to swallow is that there may not be an opportunity to reconcile some relationships, but that should not stop us from doing what we can with the ones that we still have access to. This is not to say that all relationships need to be restored. Some relationships were birthed out of premature or immature decisions and might be best to leave inactive, but this is the exception not the rule.

Reconciliation presents a picture of bringing something back to its original condition or state. It often enters into the dark realm of unforgiveness to retrieve the fragmented pieces of relationships that have been discarded. Wounds will not heal properly unless they are addressed. In fact, if the wound is not addressed, it has the potential to get worse due to infection.

There is a saying that time heals all wounds, and there is the implication that this is a passive process that only entails the balm of time to be applied in order for there to be restoration. While time may be an aid in this process, at some point, there has to be some intentional activity invoked by one of the parties involved to initiate the process of healing.

A choice has to be made by someone to determine how they are going to respond to the situation at hand.

Repairing the Sync

When we first moved into our home, one of the first things that we wanted to upgrade was our kitchen sink. It was a single, top-mounted sink that had no garbage disposal. It wasn't imperative that the style of the sink was changed immediately, but we definitely needed a garbage disposal. So, I initiated my first DIY project to install one.

Oddly enough, it was not as difficult as I anticipated, until I had to start dealing with the plumbing. Due to the size of the unit, the initial plumbing arrangement was not conducive and would need to be reconfigured. One of the most difficult aspects of this project was coupling new pieces with the existing parts. Some of the existing material had been modified so the fittings didn't always go together seamlessly. After watching several YouTube videos, taking numerous trips to the Ace Hardware store, and hours of adjusting to stop various leaks, the task was finally completed. It presented its challenges, and there were essential steps and actions that I needed to take in order for me to get my desired result.

Reconciliation can be a daunting endeavor, but the reward can outweigh the difficulty if you choose to persevere. It can involve removing old tendencies and replacing them with new habits that would better serve the relationship. You may find that there were areas that you thought were sealed, issues that you thought were resolved, but they remain inadequately repaired, allowing slow leaks of bitterness to pool. Just like repairing the sink, there will be tools and actionable steps that need to be employed to accomplish the goal. Here are a few components that are necessary:

1. Humility: This is essential to facilitate reconciliation. Whether employed by the offender or the offended, restoration of the relationship will not be able to materialize in its absence. The apology and the absolution are both offspring of humility. Being able to say "I'm sorry" for the wrong that was committed is equally as humbling as saying "I forgive you." Both

entail positioning yourself lower in this relational hierarchy for the sake of repairing the damage.

2. Desire to reconcile: This element is driven by the value that is assigned to the relationship. If the value is not seen in the relationship, then the desire to reconcile is not as prevalent. When the offense carries more weight than the value of retaining the relationship, then this desire may never arise, and reconciliation may never take place. In short, the matter of desire is impacted by the question of "Do I feel like this relationship is worth it?"

3. Clearing the ledger: Pardon the debt owed by a person in your mind. This is simply the willingness to forgive. It is drawing the line through the offense in the registry of infractions in your mind, which I don't recommend that you retain. Holding a record of wrongs and recounting an error made is a hindrance in reconciliation.

Them's Fightin' Words

A factor in facilitating reconciliation lies in the ability to manage our words. The book of Proverbs speaks extensively of being mindful of what we say. In the movie *Croods 2* there was a scene where two characters Grug and Phil Betterman were squared off in the lair of the Punch Monkeys. If you have never seen the movie, your eyebrow being raised right now is both understandable and justified. Just stay with me for a moment.

In this physical engagement, they begin to make statements about one another that seem to accelerate their fatigue. Statements like, "You built a wall around your family. You also built a wall around your heart," "Your precious pack is glad you're gone 'cause you smother them," and, in unison, "You are a bad father!" Another character, Guy, witnesses this exchange and exclaims out of this profound epiphany, "words…as weapons?!" It was in this moment that he began to recount some of the words that he said to his love interest, Eep, and realized how he had inflicted pain and caused an impact by the words that he said.[2]

---

2 Crawford, Joel, 2021. The Croods: A New Age. Universal City, CA: Universal Pictures.

Life and death are in the power of the tongue and our words have the ability to both wound and mend. I believe that the Holy Spirit can tenderize the heart of an offended individual through reminding them of the gracious words that were spoken during a dispute or the restraint from speaking words in response to the heat of the moment. The reminders of these gracious words can be like sweet honeycomb offsetting the bitter taste of unforgiveness. They are disarming.

This is more of a proactive approach, as it emphasizes always being mindful of what is being spoken. So, in the event of a disagreement, the path to reconciliation is made smoother and not as treacherous as it could've been if they were not previously considered.

PART III –
MY VIEW OF LEADERSHIP

CHAPTER 14:
Leadership is Influence

The concept of leadership intrigues and resonates within me. It intrigues me because of the profound impact that it can have on individuals, communities, and nations. The effects of leadership can determine success or failure, abundance or poverty, righteousness or depravity. It can shape culture and weave the very fabric of conscience and soul within society.

Leadership is a buzzword that is often associated with those of high rank or status, whether in a corporate business setting or in the area of government. It is a word that I think is highly misunderstood; therefore, it is misappropriated, and when something is misused, its value, or at least the perception of its value, begins to diminish. It is for this reason that I would attempt to restore the tarnished appearance of leadership and display it in its opulence, in its richness, with all that it has to offer.

Leadership Facelift

I am inspired by stories and movies that capture the loyalty and commitment exemplified by people who have been impacted by true leadership. Whether in fiction or nonfiction, I love the concept of the rally: the regrouping in the face of opposition, ushered by an individual who will lead the charge by example, willing to sacrifice all for the sake of a greater purpose. These acts strum the very heartstrings of my inner being as inspiration reverberates throughout my spirit and soul.

I remember the internal ovation that was given during the scene in *The Avengers: Endgame* movie when Captain America stood alone, battered, with a broken shield, facing Thanos and his hoard. As he received the call in his earpiece, "on your left,"[3] and began to see the multiple portals open with those united for the same purpose emerging from them, you could feel the inspiration and hope that was intended to be conveyed in the movie. The calm yet authoritative directive that was given, "Avengers... assemble," preceded the advance into one of the most satisfying cinematic battles I have seen. So, let us also proceed in our advance into understanding this concept of leadership.

In order to initiate this process of re-presenting leadership, I think that it is necessary to discuss how leadership is defined, at least, how I perceive leadership is defined, since this book is about my perspective. My definition of leadership has been derived from several sources, including living examples, experiences, and authors. The springboard of my understanding of leadership can be found in a statement from James Hunter's book *The Servant*. It stated that "Leadership is the skill of influencing people to work enthusiastically towards goals identified as being for the common good."[4]

The key point in that statement is that leadership is about influence. Let me take a moment to define influence. Influence is making an impression. The impact of one thing that leaves its indentation or mark of itself on another. It is like sitting in a seat and the pressure of your body weight leaving a dent in the seat cushion. The seat cushion has now contoured or has been shaped by the weight of your presence. This is a visual representation of the nature of influence.

Leadership refers to the pre-set, well-established character which provides the needed model to direct others. It is positively impacting them by example. In the book of Romans, an exhortation is presented that we "lead with diligence" (12:8 AMP). Being diligent to take the lead underlines the effectiveness of influencing people by having a respected reputation, one built on a solid "track-record."

---

3   Russo, Anthony, and Joe Russon, 2019. Avengers: Endgame. United States: Walt Disney Studios Motion Pictures.
4   James C. Hunter, *The Servant: A Simple Story about the True Essence of Leadership* (New York: Crown Business., 2012).

So, how does one gain influence? By **modeling character**, becoming a **master of consistency,** and **maintaining competency**, which I will discuss later on. Leadership is the state or condition of influencing people to action in such a way that inspires confidence and produces excellence. At its core, it is about discovering or recognizing potential and helping to actualize it in a person's life.

We are Salt

"You are the salt of the earth, but if salt has lost its taste, how shall its saltiness be restored?" (Matthew 5:13). I love hamburgers. Yes, I know that seems like a displaced statement in light of this conversation, but hear me out. I am constantly in search of a delectable hamburger. If I am traveling, I seek out the best burger restaurant that I can find.

One of my pet peeves is when I order a burger and it is presented in excellence, dressed exquisitely with complimentary toppings, cooked to the point that there is still a little pink that is visible and appears to model perfection, only to be nullified by the lack of flavor in the meat itself, bland. The only thing saving the burger are the toppings meant to compliment not to be the primary focus. I often comment that if they would've just put some salt in the meat, then it would've enhanced the flavor of the beef.

Saltiness is the unique quality and characteristic associated with salt. It helps identify and define it. Without this quality, the use or operation of the salt becomes modified. Its intended purpose is not fulfilled. Although salt can have different uses, Jesus emphasizes its characteristic of flavor. Saltiness is associated with seasoning, enhancing the flavor of the food. If salt does not do this, then it provides no added value to the food.

So, within the identity of the salt, its purpose finds its context. Since saltiness is an intrinsic quality of salt, it goes to say that its existence envelopes its purpose. It was made for the purpose of enhancement and adding flavor. So it is with us. Since we were created in the image of God, with the unique quality of His nature, including the ability to influence, then we are born to bring influence and lead. We were created and born to bring enhancement to whatever we encounter.

Is Leadership a Skill?

I have heard it said that leadership is a skill. I do not wholly endorse this statement because of the definition of skill. Skill is defined as the "ability to do something well; expertise." Although this can be a matter of semantics, I think that it is necessary to address because there are several people that think that they are unable to be leaders because they feel like they lack the ability or skill to do so.

Some people believe that there are some who are born leaders, possessing this innate capacity to effectively manage and lead groups to achieving collective goals. This is interesting because while I believe that everyone was born to lead, I also believe that leadership and management are two different things. These two terms are often used interchangeably resulting in a patchwork understanding of what leadership is.

I subscribe to the idea that the term "manager" is a role, and the term "leader" is an identity. Management tends to revolve around the administration of tasks, overseeing the execution until their completion. Leadership, however, addresses the condition of the person by whom the tasks will be completed, thus impacting the manner and quality in which they are done. Management is task-focused while leadership is people-focused.

While I don't believe that leadership itself is a skill, I believe that there are skills that need to be developed in order to bolster, accentuate, or extend the amount of influence that you have. To illustrate, leadership is like an aroma or a fragrance. It is the byproduct or the result produced by the very nature of something. It is released from the makeup or composition.

When a fragrance or an aroma fills the room, it impacts all of those who are in it. Now just like a flower intrinsically has what is needed to produce the aroma, within our composition lies the elements needed to produce true leadership. Respectively, there are also methods that can be applied or used to enhance or extract what already exists.

Think of leadership as being a matter of posture. We are all born with the innate ability to stand or the potential to stand. What impacts posture is awareness. So, what is to be considered is not whether we can stand, but the manner in which we are standing.

Have you ever found yourself slouching? What do you normally do next? In most cases, once you are aware, you adjust and stand up straight, right? The awareness brought the adjustment. If leadership is about influence, your awareness of the influence that you have will cause you to adjust, just as you would when you slouch. The correction is supported by understanding that your posture, your stance, can have an impact on the body or the environment that you find yourself in.

My intention is not to make this concept too abstract, but really it is to encourage that being a leader is not exclusive to a particular group or certain type of person. It is a universally, equal opportunity available to all if viewed through the correct lens.

CHAPTER 15:
The Misconceptions of Leadership

As implied, I have an uncommon view that everyone was born to lead. This is an audacious statement that has and, undoubtedly, will be scrutinized. However, the criticism derives and draws from a well of misconception. Most of what we've been taught about leadership revolves around self: self-preservation, self-exaltation, self-esteem or affirmation, and self-interest.

We have been taught that leadership is about control, superiority, manipulation, and popularity. Our perspective about leadership must be renewed for it to produce the fruit that it is intended. Leadership is about service, empowerment, inspiration, and pursuing purpose.

The Tale of Two Leadership Mindsets

In the Gospel of Matthew, King Herod's response was recorded after he received the news that the foretold Messiah had arrived. I would like to contrast King Herod's response with that of John the Baptist, who also received similar news. Both men were faced with the reality that their position or status had the potential to change, but they had two totally different reactions.

King Herod, knowing and believing that there was a coming Messiah, was moved by selfish ambition and arrogance to murder the Christ to maintain his status. The message of a forthcoming King would mean that his reign would be superseded, and the thought of his kingdom being supplanted was one too difficult to entertain. He was willing to commit a great atrocity and inflict inconsolable pain on many for the sake of maintaining his position.

In contrast, when John the Baptist was informed that Jesus was gaining notoriety, his response was "I am filled with joy at his success. He must become greater and greater, and I must become less and less" (John 3:30 NLT). John did not become insecure, try to reinvent his image, or rebrand himself so that he could maintain his celebrity. He did not attempt to compete by heralding his role as the forerunner to the Messiah. He took pleasure in what Jesus had been able to achieve. He did not dismiss his function, but he also did not elevate it to a place where it caused him to overlook the grand scheme.

Both men were in positions of leadership. Both of their distinct views of leadership were made evident in the manner in which they responded. The true nature and quality of their perspectives were revealed: one that highlighted selfishness while the other emphasized humility.

Leadership is about ~~Control~~...Service

Everyone wants to be in control. Control implies fulfillment of one's agenda or will. Having control means that there is something or someone subject to your dictates, orders, commands, or requirements. Control is naturally a result of leadership, but it should not be the pursuit in leadership. When control is the pursuit in leadership, it creates a dictatorial mindset.

Micromanaging tends to find itself entrenched within this state of mind. The strings of the marionette will not be relinquished and simply choreographing will not satiate. It is not uncharacteristic for those chasing after control to concern themselves only with their own needs. The needs of others are lost in oblivion as personal welfare is often elevated to top priority.

True leadership is about service. It is tending to the condition of others, extending support to reach resolution, and offering the assistance needed to excel. In my role as a manager, I made it my aim to supply my team with the tools and resources necessary for them to complete the objectives that I set out. I also made sure that I presented myself as an advocate for them when they did not have the bandwidth. This, of course, would only be profitable if I possessed the capability or had the competence to adequately provide reinforcement.

Now, there may be apprehension with taking this active role because of the fear of creating unhealthy dependency, but I view it as establishing a safety net. Most people would be more willing to walk on a tightrope if they had security below to catch them if there was a misstep. My efforts were motivated by my desire for them to succeed.

In most hierarchical pyramids, a leader is normally at the top and not the bottom. Leadership is not often associated with support or foundation. A dispute arose amongst the disciples of Jesus regarding who of them was the greatest. Who was the most significant and carried the most impact? Jesus' response was one that shifted the paradigm on how leadership was perceived. He explained that most view leadership in terms of lording over others and are lauded as philanthropists or doers of good.

"The kings of the Gentiles exercise lordship over them, and those in authority over them are called benefactors" (Luke 22:25 ESV). There is an expectation of prestige, bestowed honor and recognition, that is commonly associated with leadership and tends to be the appeal of being in such positions. However, a diametrically different point of view was offered in regard to how leadership should be perceived. "...But not so with you. Rather, let the greatest among you become as the youngest, and the leader as the one who serves" (Luke 22:26 ESV).

What a foreign concept. This notion suggested that leaders should be clothed in a garment of humility instead of being adorned in the fabric of high regard. This was a challenge in both perception and application. This concept is not about thinking less of yourself in regard to value but thinking of yourself less in regard to accommodation.

Leadership is about ~~Superiority~~...Empowerment

When leadership is misunderstood, the terrain of misunderstanding becomes a breeding ground for insecurity. When coupled with position or title, this can result in a superiority complex. Someone finds their significance in a title and now feels like they are greater than others because of it.

One who is insecure will never empower because they fear that it will diminish their value. So, they will intentionally neglect to invest in others through training, sharing knowledge, and asking others for ideas and feedback. Unbeknownst to them, by maintaining this posture of fists tightly clenched, unwilling to give of what they have in their hands, they are preventing themselves from receiving anything more as well. It is just as much a detriment to them as it is to those around them.

Empowerment is partnering to equip. This is not only delegation of authority, but also conveyance of confidence and support that enables the recipient to discover solutions on their own. I can recall having a conversation with one of my employees, and he was communicating some issues that other employees were expressing to him.

I noticed how it was becoming a weight on him. He was fervent about their plight, but also overwhelmed by the burden that he was carrying. My advice to him was that it was not his responsibility to carry everybody's cross. Absorbing the problems of everyone else while not encouraging them to participate was not only adding strain to himself, but also disabling them from being able to resolve them in the future.

I was not encouraging him to reposition to indifference on the opposite side of the spectrum, but rather to come alongside the people that he wanted to help and provide the balance necessary to create stability. Empowerment is about getting people to believe and embrace that they are able and capable of accomplishing something. It is making them cognizant that they have the permission to be exceptional.

Leadership is about ~~Manipulation~~...Inspiration

"Whoever wishes to be great among you must be your servant" (Mark 10:43 NASB). Before I begin on this next concept, let me rephrase this statement to make it more personal so the context is not misconstrued. This statement does not imply that you advertise the promise of greatness if someone comes and serves you. Au contraire, it is saying that if "YOU" desire greatness, humility on your part is required and the aim or goal should be to empower the next.

Our society tends to praise being cunning or crafty, but it is not to the benefit of our society. It takes advantage. Manipulation is a form of persuasion; however, the motives and purposes are not ethical, moral, or principled. It is deceptive to achieve its own agenda.

Manipulation is skillful in nature because it analyzes how to get someone to react or respond, usually catering to selfish ambition. It does not consider the interests of others; therefore, its actions can actually cause harm to individuals. When leadership is associated with or viewed as being manipulative, it can cause one to undermine authority. Due to their unwillingness to be manipulated, they can refuse to come under the authority of another, therefore disqualifying themselves from having authority of their own.

Inspiration encourages development or advancement in a particular area. Inspiration leads to progress, forward momentum, and fulfillment. Leaders inspire because their focus is gaining new ground that they can bring their influence to. It is the expansion of excellence through esteeming those in your environment.

My wife and I were conversing, and she made mention of key people in her life that encouraged her to go beyond what was expected. While she was content and found it acceptable to operate in the mundane, they would highlight her potential to access the extraordinary. (I got her permission to discuss this, by the way.) My wife is gifted in the area of teaching and has a plethora of knowledge that can be served in a way that is easily digestible due to her ability. Notwithstanding, a gift can remain unenjoyed if it stays in the package. While these voices in her life cannot assume full credit as the sole catalyst, they were absolutely instrumental in changing her life's trajectory.

The role of a leader is to extract the gold that is embedded within individuals and help them to present it to the world. Everyone has something to offer. It is a unique contribution that God has given us the privilege to bestow; sometimes we just need the help to identify what it is.

Leadership is about Pursuing ~~Popularity~~... Purpose _____

It is a common concept now to pursue followers. On our social media accounts, the primary objective is to see how many followers we can amass. People are deemed "influencers" when they reach a certain number of followers or fans. So now we tend to equate leadership with the number of fans we obtain.

Lecrae Moore stated, "If we live by people's acceptance, then we will die by their rejection."[5] If your pursuit as a leader is popularity and being accepted or liked, then you will risk compromising things of value such as honor, compassion, and integrity. This does not mean to be indifferent or seek out ways to offend people because you don't care whether they accept you or not. I read that "tact is the art of making a point without making an enemy." There is a way to get your point across without being offensive.

Dan Mohler has been a voice in my life, as well as my wife's, for about a decade. He is an itinerant pastor that readily admits that he is not tech savvy. As he would go and preach the good news of the Kingdom, he would not post videos, he did not have a social media account, and he did not advertise his ministry. You may ask, "Well, how did you hear about him?" Fair question. People were so inspired by him and the way that he presented the gospel that they would capture his messages and post them online.

He gained a following, but it wasn't because he sought it out. He was consistent in his message which aligned to the consistency in his life and caused him to gain influence. His goal was to present the unadulterated gospel in its simplicity and to show its effectual nature demonstrated through the manner in which he lived his life.

Leaders pursue purpose. Purpose is the "why," the motivation, the vision, the horsepower that drives your actions. Purpose is like the baton within your possession that reminds you of why you are running so hard. Without it, the race can seem meaningless.

"When there is no clear prophetic vision, people quickly wander astray" (Proverbs 29:18 TPT). Life can take on the semblance and redun-

---

5   Lecrae (@lecrae), "If we live by people's acceptance, then we will die by their rejection." Twitter. August 14, 2012.

dancy of a hamster wheel when there is no definitive target or clear directive. Wandering may seem benign, but if it characterizes your life, then it is an indication that purpose is not being pursued. We were not created to grasp for wind and lay hold of no substance.

Success in Succession

These misconceptions about leadership can also rob from one of the fruits of true leadership which is successful succession. Succession is the perpetuation of purpose. How can longevity be obtained without someone to administer or carry on the purpose? When there is a failure to invest in succession, there is an acceleration of decay within that group, organization, or nation. The decay impacts the culture and can cause it to deteriorate to the point of ruin.

In my professional career, it was common for the tenure to exceed twenty years at our company. People were dedicated and truly valued the company, in large part, because the company valued them. With long tenure comes a lot of experience and knowledge, which is beneficial, unless it is not passed on.

There came a point in time when many of those seasoned employees were ready to retire, and there was a mass exodus at one time. This, inevitably, left a void that we feverishly tried to fill. We literally were collectively losing hundreds of years of knowledge and experience. How can that be backfilled? This obviously created difficulties in various areas of quality and customer service, not due to indifference, but inexperience. In hindsight, I can tell you that prevention of this occurrence can only happen proactively. To fortify the future, there has to be a deliberate investment in the bridge that connects the seasoned and the blossoming, the established and the innovative, the experienced and the aspiring.

CHAPTER 16:
Branches of Leadership

I have mentioned all three of these previously, but I would like to explore in more depth how these three aspects are keys to exemplifying true leadership. Look at these aspects as being branches. Branches are the mediums to express what the vine within them are producing. If the fruit being produced is influence, then these branches are the extensions that would make the fruit available at greater lengths.

Modeling Character

What is the point of a model? It is to show or display as an example or template. It is a springboard from which ideas are catapulted or a reference that is used for the purpose of replicating. I would venture to say that there are certain qualities such as genuineness, sincerity, and honor that could stand to be imitated in our society.

The very roots of leadership are securely fastened in the foundation of character. Character speaks at a higher decibel level than words alone could produce. When I think of someone with proven character, two words come to mind: integrity and excellence. "A good name is to be chosen rather than great riches, and favor is better than silver and gold" (Proverbs 22:1 ESV).

A good name or a good reputation is often associated with the display of integrity. Doing what's known to be right, even and especially when no one is watching. Integrity is also the willingness to accept accountability, which is simply taking ownership. If I have the willingness to receive the credit and accolades of a task completed well, then I must also have the courage to readily accept the responsibility when I have made a mistake.

I have subscribed to this definition for years, but I don't think that I considered the significance of the inconspicuous quality of integrity. It highlights motive. What is being done is not for show or to gain recognition or a pat on the back. It is being done out of identity and in excellence. It is also keeping your word. Doing what you say that you are going to do. I do not know if there is any greater establishment or hindrance to trust than in the area of integrity.

The phrase "my word is my bond" has been used throughout the years to convey the message of the value of integrity. It was used by maritime brokers and merchant traders to make agreements that were legally binding without written documents. You can imagine, to renege would have ramifications whose impact would be multifaceted. To have an untrustworthy reputation would affect the business that you were trying to conduct, which would ultimately affect your income and means to provide for yourself and family. This same concept still holds true and has an impact on the potential reach of your influence.

Maintaining Competency

Your level of competence will also help determine how far the influence of your leadership will reach. Skills such as communication, resourcefulness, and technique are all necessary to be a successful leader. Your competence level is also a source of confidence that will be established in your team.

While I do believe in the adage that "people don't care about how much you know until they know how much you care," I will add that once they know how much you care, they are going to be interested in how much you know. Competence comes with intentionality and commitment. One does not become skilled in an area by accident nor through indifference.

I enjoy working out and playing chess. Over the years, I have gleaned a harvest of insight through my engagement in both activities. With exercising, primarily lifting weights, I learned that stagnation can easily beset me, and my muscles would plateau at a certain size and strength level if I did not push myself to incrementally add more weight or perform more repetitions. It is easy to become complacent when you are able to perform at the current state that you are in.

When I stopped exercising for a period, I learned that it became more difficult for me to get started again, until my body started reflecting a shape that more resembled the Stay Puft Marshmallow Man. At that point, once I began exercising again, the place where I was once confident or comfortable was now a challenge. Resting on your laurels will not promote advancement, and if there is no intentionality in keeping your skills sharpened, then just like a knife, they will become dull after continuous use.

What I learned from chess is the need for strategy development, especially if I played the same opponent. What would happen is that if I continued to use the same strategy, my opponent would become aware of that strategy and know how to easily counter it. If I did not take the time to learn and employ a new strategy or method, then I faced more losses than victories. Not only did the frequency of the losses increase, but the time that it took for me to lose decreased. So, I was getting beaten faster and more often.

In the same way, if I am not committed to sharpening my skills in the area that I am engaged in, I will find that my success rate will begin to decrease. Why? It is because to grow and maintain success, change is not simply inevitable, it is essential. Having a cavalier or casual approach to competency can be the cause of missed opportunities and lead to ambiguity amongst your team.

Mastering Consistency

Successful leadership is evident when mastering consistency. Consistency brings consolation to those around you because it is stable. It gives people something to count on. I worked under the supervision of an individual that I was never sure of what version of the person I was going to encounter on a given day. I didn't know if I was going to encounter the jovial, affable side or the micromanaging, vindictive side. It made it difficult to navigate and affected productivity, at some level, because I needed to assess the climate.

Sometimes, I had to be strategic about how I accomplished a task because the method that I employed may not have been suitable on a given day, based on how the individual was feeling. Sounds exhausting, right? Without consistency, it is difficult to establish the pillars that are essential to developing a successful team. The person that we consistently show ourselves to be is going to determine the level of influence that we will obtain. In the marriage of competence and character, consistency is the adhesive that enables you to thrive as a leader.

CHAPTER 17:
Compound Influence

While I do not profess a proclivity in the area of finance, I found myself drawn to the concept of compound interest and how it could be correlated to the concept of influence. It led me to manufacture this concept of "compound influence" that I would like to introduce to you. In the simplest of terms, compound interest occurs when interest gets added to the principal amount invested or borrowed, and then the interest rate applies to the new, larger principal. Over time it can lead to exponential growth.

Like compound interest, the concept of compound influence revolves around the idea that substantial growth occurs in the form of impact and influence when perspective change (interest rate) is applied to the person (principal). To maximize the fruit of this investment, it is most expedient to start early. This is why the leadership mentality should be instilled at the point of entry instead of when a position becomes available. The effects will be more far reaching this way. It is the amount of influence that occurs due to true leadership.

As the paradigm shifts in the area of leadership, the greater the influence will expand. Your words and input will retain greater value, not because you inherently have more value than someone else, but because your reputation has preceded you. Your character has been established and vouched for; therefore, your credibility has been solidified. This influence can have a profound impact on your environment and those around you.

For example, there have been several people that were gainfully employed or given more consideration based on my recommendation. That may come off as prideful or arrogant, but that is not the intention. I simply recognize that in modeling character, mastering consistency, and maintaining competency, a foundation has been established for me that has allowed me to make suggestions that were strongly considered and oftentimes adhered to. I strongly believe that had I not demonstrated these tenets, I would not have been able to help the people that I have been privileged to help over the years.

I often use the analogy that a ripple can turn into a tidal wave. This idea echoes the concept of the "butterfly effect theory," the phenomenon whereby a minute localized change in a complex system can have large effects elsewhere. I believe that small elements, seemingly miniscule and insignificant shifts, can have lasting impact. "See how great a forest a little fire kindles" (James 3:5 NKJV).

The Impact of Leadership

True leadership promotes, guides, and directs into purpose. True leaders keep the target at the forefront, as a reminder of what is being pursued and why the effort is being enforced. The expression of my leadership is yielded from what I perceive a leader to be and inevitably impacts how I operate in whatever role that I have been assigned. I have seen the aftermath of both true leadership and poor leadership, and my conclusion is that they are equally transformative. The weight that leadership carries can be understated, and the effects are not always immediately evident, but do not be deceived into thinking that it is restricted access to the multifaceted areas of life, business, family, and society.

PART IV -
MY VIEW OF SUCCESS

CHAPTER 18:
The Value of a Journey

One of our common pursuits as human beings is the pursuit of success. In our own experiences, we may feel like we have achieved a level of success. Others may feel like it's been the proverbial dangling carrot that is run after, but unable to be captured. Most people will admit that they want success, but what is success?

Can you define it? If you can't define it, how do you pursue it? How will you know if it's been caught? I would like to propose that success is not a one-time event or destination, but it is a dynamic, ongoing journey.

When we are trying to get to a certain destination, whether it be metaphorically or literally, most times we would like to instantly be there. Would you agree? I think that we want to skip the journey because we often consider it to be synonymous with hardships, which I don't necessarily believe is true. Hardships may come while on the journey, but the journey itself should not be defined by adversity.

I think that the journey is essential to appreciate the destination. A journey takes time, and time is our most valuable asset. So, when that asset is traded in exchange for the voyage, the destination becomes that much more valuable.

Another element that can be constituted as an important part of a journey is the confidence that is developed in your guide. When your guide is able to lead you to your destination, then your trust in that guide is cultivated and advancement becomes the natural progression. In my life, the Holy Spirit is that guide, that navigator. While I may be stationed at the helm on the ship of my life having the volition to steer the way, I rely on my navigator who provides the most expedient course.

In His counsel, He considers the obstacles and storms that can be encountered along with the reward and satisfaction that comes with the completion of the endeavor. I am not of the persuasion that hardships come as a ploy from God, but rather as a deterrent from the enemy, in the attempt to disrupt the relationship with God and to deviate from purpose. However, it is through those hardships that God will further solidify His standing as a trustworthy guide, never losing sight of the terminus.

Target Acquired

Success is determined, defined, or characterized by what your target is. Your purpose is what substantiates your success, meaning that the fulfillment of your purpose is the metric of your success. As you continue to fulfill your purpose, hitting your target, so to speak, you will find yourself walking in success.

Success can be subjective because each of us has a purpose or reason for our existence; therefore, my definition of success can be different from the next person's. One of the key errors that we experience is not being aware of this fact; therefore, we begin to measure our success by the success of others, unaware that we may be comparing apples to oranges. If our targets are different, if our goals are different, then the outcomes cannot be measured the same way.

Another error is confusing being accomplished with being successful. Someone can be accomplished, in that they have achieved renown, executed and completed many assignments, and accumulated material wealth. This does not automatically equate to being successful. I'm sure that on many trains of thought, what I have described are adequate gauges for success. However, I believe that our success is in direct relation to our purpose.

Myles Munroe wrote, "Life's greatest failure is to be successful in the wrong assignment."[6] Imagine that you were charged to construct an aq-

6   Munroe, Myles. *Kingdom principles: Preparing for Kingdom experience and expansion.* Shippensburg, PA: Destiny Image Publishers, 2006.

ueduct from one place to provide water to another area. You built the structure, but the conduit leads in the wrong direction. So here, you accomplished the task of constructing the aqueduct, but it was going to an incorrect location, so the purpose was not fulfilled. It was not successful.

Another example would be trying to use a fork to rake leaves. If employed, the fork would be able to accomplish the task. It would be painstaking, laborious and time consuming, but it could be done. Would that be considered a success? I would have to give that a thumbs down. Why? It is because the fork was not used for its intended purpose. Therefore, the use of its time wasn't properly utilized and the level of efficiency in which it was operating was not optimized.

So, the question that has to be asked is, "What or who is determining your purpose?" Is it the media? Social acceptance? Your parents? God? What is your target? Answering this is paramount because it will then dictate how you live your life and give a more accurate metric of your level of success.

CHAPTER 19:
Pliable Structure

Success has to be defined in our lives, but we also need to allow space for adjustments to be made. We have to be flexible to redefine what success may look like at different stages of our lives. My modus operandi tends to consist of this concept that I will call "pliable structure." I like to begin with an established plan, so that anarchy will not ensue; however, I do not want to be so rigid that any deviation from that plan is discarded and considered inconsequential because it was not the original.

This malleable approach has various applications in both personal and professional realms. It is antonymous to the "my way or the highway" mentality that gives no room for change, adaptation, or modification. It is also not an ally to the notion of rolling the dice and seeing what happens. It is drawing a blueprint with a pencil and an eraser, affording the ability to make changes if needed.

With keeping our target in mind, it is essential to realize that success, in relation to our purpose, can take on different forms and expressions at various points in time. For example, my overarching purpose is to be an ambassador of Christ, thus fulfilling the will of my King to advance His Kingdom on this earth. My success in fulfilling this purpose was expressed differently as a single man in distinction to when I married my wife and had children.

The areas of my involvement had to be reassessed due to my priorities being shifted. Attending events or participating in ventures that did not necessarily indicate a finite conclusion were no longer as suitable as they may have been before. In addition, the manner of my representation now had the opportunity to be conveyed through the lens of unbridled commitment and fidelity. I had the chance to demonstrate what a healthy, Heavenly Kingdom-oriented family could look like.

The takeaway from this is that success goes through periods of evolution. Here is a good picture: Think about a relay race where diverse actions need to be employed in order to finish the race. You may need to run, swim, carry an egg in a spoon, jump in a knapsack...I think you get the picture. The ultimate goal is to get across the finish line, but there are different methods at various stages of the race that are employed in order to be successful in the competition. At each stage, the level of success was measured by the completion utilizing the designated method. So, while measuring success, it is imperative that your season of life is factored in.

CHAPTER 20:
Circumstantial Slavery

Would you agree that many of our actions have been contingent upon our external conditions? Are we impelled by circumstances instead of being motivated by purpose? "Do you not know that if you continually surrender yourselves to anyone to do his will, you are the slaves of him whom you obey…?" (Romans 6:16 AMPC).

Slavery is characterized by the lack of control, options, and the ability to make your own decision. It is a hopeless and despairing state that only cultivates one desire: escape. The slave's primary purpose of existence is to acquiesce to the demands and serve the needs of the slave owner. No questions asked. At the expense of the slave's well-being, emotional state, belief system, et cetera, the slave owner's interests are paramount in this system.

In the concept of slavery, the slave has no choice. They must answer every beck and call, in the fear that failure to do so will result in reprimand. A slave's life is reactive since their actions are solely a result of the instruction they have been given by their master. Their master tells them what and when to eat, where to go, and what to do.

Now, in an effort to lighten this somber topic, as I was watching the Disney movie *Aladdin* (I'm a fan of the animated version, though the live action version starring Will Smith is starting to grow on me), one of the parts that sticks out is Aladdin's conversation with the genie. Aladdin asks the genie what he would wish for, and his wish was simple: freedom. The idea of being his own master, making his own decisions, having a choice was a dream to him.

Spoiler alert for those who have never seen *Aladdin*, there was a tender moment at the end of the movie when Aladdin makes his final wish to set Genie free. The possibilities, the potential, and the opportunities inundated the Genie's mind. Ideas that were once incomprehensible were now tangible, and it was exciting and exhilarating.

Why am I talking about slaves, slave owners, and Aladdin? The answer is simple: it is because we have all been enslaved at some point in our lives. Some of us are still being enslaved by a common slave owner: our circumstances.

Can you recall being in a certain situation and it dictating every decision that you made and every action that you performed? It occupied your mind to the point where the majority of your thoughts revolved around it. You were consumed by it, ready to adhere to its every command. You may have resigned to such notions as, "These are just the cards that life has dealt me." or "It is what it is." As I am writing this, I find myself in the midst of a circumstance that is trying its best to keep me bound in slavery, but I have discovered the key to my freedom and am determined to experience it. I will discuss what this key is, but I think that it is necessary to prime before divulging.

The Precoat

Priming is a good word to use here. When I think of priming, I refer to the process of painting. Priming is a preparatory coat that is applied before you paint something. Its purpose is to provide an increased cohesion of the paint to the surface. It helps the paint cling to the object that it is being applied to more effectively.

In my own life, I have realized that I have missed reaching success in some areas because I was not willing to be primed. I did not persevere through the process of preparation that would allow the truths that were being administered to me to actually cling to my life and enjoy the benefits of them. I wanted the end result. I just wanted the surface painted, not realizing that the "paint" being applied would not be an adequate cover and there would be a lot of the old surface showing through.

I know that I'm speaking in a lot of metaphors here, but in a nutshell, I believe that a shift in heart and mind needs to take place before I convey an answer to this problem of enslavement. If the perspective change does not take place, then the answer can be disheartening and discouraging.

Shallow Ground

Jesus describes a scenario like this when he describes the Kingdom of Heaven being like a seed that is scattered onto shallow ground. The seed immediately springs up because there is no depth of soil; however, when the sun comes out, the plant is scorched and withers because it didn't have much root. What is being conveyed is that the seed is a truth that is revealed to the heart of a person. The person is zealous and receives it with joy but does not give the truth the opportunity to be cultivated in their heart.

It is not given a chance to grow and produce an enduring faith, a confidence in what God has already accomplished and in who He is. So, when opposition, the circumstances that are contrary to the revealed truth, begin to surface, the person retreats or is burned out and discouraged. The truth is lost or invalidated in that person's mind now.

Be Free

The greatest foe to success is the lie that "there is nothing that can be done." It weakens the wind in your sails and places the chains of circumstantial serfdom upon you. This type of thinking is the precursor to slavery. It is the introduction to a life and system that I discussed earlier, where we are all trying to escape from.

I have often challenged the perspective of those who I've managed, to look at a situation and consider "how it can be done?" instead of asserting "why it can't be done." When challenges arise, we tend to take the wide and broad road most traveled which is retreating to that place of refuge where we can be justified in our inaction by the claim that it was just out of our control. This place is void of accountability and ownership, and this place of "refuge" is actually a guise for a place of captivity.

Well, I want to proclaim freedom to the captives. I want to convey that confinement by your circumstance is not the intention for your life, but it will take a change of perspective to get released. The question is are you willing? I think that willingness is just as important as execution, sometimes more.

To illustrate, I was watching a show called *The Chosen*, and there was a scene where a man afflicted with leprosy was coming to see Jesus. What struck me and had the most impact was the man crying, asking Jesus if He was willing to make him clean, pleading with Him "don't turn away from me."[7] The scene adequately captured the sincerity of the moment.

I think that Jesus' willingness to make him clean had just as much impact as His ability to administer the healing to the man. Willingness shows desire and produces confidence in the fulfillment of something. I am much more confident that I will receive a gift or a promise when I know that the benefactor actually wants to give it to me.

---

7   Jenkins, Dallas, director. The Chosen. Season 1, episode 6. "Indescribable Compassion."

CHAPTER 21:
Challenges: Opportunities or Excuses

I believe that our reactions or responses are products of our perspective, so you can often identify your perspective by how you initially respond to a situation. What is normally your first reaction to a challenge or an inconvenience? Do you see it as an opportunity or an excuse?

My focus is to help you become aware of your reaction to inconveniences or challenges, so that you can determine if a shift in your perspective about them is needed. To provide more clarity, let's define opportunities and excuses. Simply put, an opportunity is a chance to grow or advance, whereas an excuse is a reason to justify lack of growth or advancement. When challenges arise, there are a few stages that we tend to go through:

Intake - we are given the information.

Process - we filter the information through our perception.

Complain or solve - we respond.

After the information is given, the processing begins. How we perceive will determine how we process, which impacts what we produce. What we produce is a reflection of how we perceive. When a challenge arises, I get to make a choice if I am going to view this as an opportunity or as an excuse. The option that I choose will determine if I will begin to complain or resolve.

So, the question that we ask ourselves is, "What are we producing?" Are we producing complaints or creating solutions? In contrasting both responses, complaining can be characterized by the proclivity to focus on what is wrong instead of what is right or what can't be done instead of what can be done. If complaining is the initial response, then challenges can be viewed as an excuse for failure, lack of growth, or stagnation.

On the opposite end of the spectrum, solving is about finding an answer. The solution-driven response is propelled by the concept that the problem is only to be acknowledged, not to be esteemed. In other words, we are not to dismiss that an issue exists, but we don't surrender the deed of our mental real estate to the problem when that time and energy can be used to come up with an answer.

I can recall several conversations and meetings where a known problem was brought up, and, like a broken record, it was reiterated over…and over…and over. It may have been restated in several ways, but nonetheless it was the same item with different packaging. At the end of the conversation, or tirade, depending on how impassioned the individual was, no definitive course of action was decided, and the same frustration and anxiety that existed prior remained. In my estimation, it was fruitless and only accentuated the difficulty that was already evident.

When we treat challenges as opportunities, it builds character and minimizes anxiety. Character is who you choose to be, and it helps you become an example amongst others around you. While this may be perceived as an oversimplification, it stands to reason that should the focus be on the solution instead of the problem, the anxiety would fade because anxiety truly comes from magnifying the problem.

The greatest detriment to not living according to the operating system of the Kingdom of God is the risk of not fully realizing your purpose. Once there is an acceptance that we have more control than what we may have been taught and that we don't have to be victims of our circumstances, it shifts the responsibility, and we come face to face with the reality that our state is a direct result of what we are believing. The excuses are invalidated. This is the key to freedom from circumstantial slavery and the catalyst for stepping onto the path of success through the fulfillment of purpose.

CHAPTER 22:
Big Picture

I have wrestled with the tendency to look at what I have "in hand" instead of what is "at hand." Jesus said, "Repent, for the Kingdom of Heaven is at hand" (Matthew 3:2 ESV). He was making a declaration of what was available: the Kingdom or government of Heaven, the resources of Heaven and all of its benefits.

It was a statement to direct our attention to look at a realm that was spiritually based that would yield tangible results. As opposed to only considering what was "in hand," which normally has the implication to focus on what is lacking. When I focus on what I have in hand, I tend to point out all the holes and deficiencies. I look at what I don't have instead of what is available.

In my field of work, we would utilize an inventory management system that indicates what inventory we have available and what inventory has already been allocated to fulfill orders. The allocated field is identified as committed. Let's say that I have an order for ten units of an item, but I am looking at the system and see that ten pieces have already been committed. If I stop there, then it would appear that I will not be able to fulfill my order. What I need has already been allocated for use.

However, if I look at what is on hand, what is actually accessible, I would realize that there are 100 units available, meaning that I have more than enough to fulfill my order. In the Kingdom of God, we have more than enough, but the experience of this truth is only realized through our choice to recognize it as being true. It is called faith.

Gazing

I have stared through many windows. They represent different stages of my life. What I saw each time was different not only because of the location, but because of the perspective and focus that I had at each time.

For example, I have looked through the windows of a naval recruiting bus. I saw that I was moving away from everything that was familiar to me, entering into a time that I was uncertain about and scared because I was alone. I have looked through the windows of jail and prison. I saw how I had given away my physical freedom, and I was aware of my separation from it. I also saw through those windows the hope that one day I would be reunited with that freedom and the ones that I loved.

I have looked through the windows of my parents' house, longing for the opportunity to stand on my own two feet and yearning to meet my lifelong companion. I have looked through the windows of our apartment, wanting to add more permanence to our home because our residence was void of furniture. I have stared through the window of my office, realizing that I never imagined myself standing in the position that I am in. I also am looking out the window, settled in the truth that my Father knows what I need and He is by my side, refusing to leave me.

Our attention, our focus is a target and prize to be won, so to speak. There are several suitors that are vying for our attention, and the first thing that we must realize is that we have the ability to determine who will receive this prize. Why is our attention and focus so valuable? It is because we become and pursue what we give our attention to. We support, defend, and advance that which we afford our attention because we have become committed to it. So, I hope that this book has inspired you to take another glance at what you believe and allow it to be cross examined.

www.ingramcontent.com/pod-product-compliance
Lightning Source LLC
Chambersburg PA
CBHW051432090426
42737CB00014B/2935